Frog Friends

by Megan Litwin
illustrated by Sheila Bailey

PEARSON

Scott
Foresman

Editorial Offices: Glenview, Illinois • Parsippany, New Jersey • New York, New York
Sales Offices: Needham, Massachusetts • Duluth, Georgia • Glenview, Illinois
Coppell, Texas • Ontario, California • Mesa, Arizona

It was a beautiful summer day at the pond. Danny, a green tree frog, was enjoying the sounds of summer from his perch atop a tall tree. Down in the pond below, his friend Fred, a bullfrog, sat near the water. Fred was waiting for his lunch.

Just then a fly crawled near Fred. Fred's long, sticky tongue shot out in a flash and caught the tiny insect.

"Delicious! I'm full now," he said loudly. He had already eaten three other insects and a worm in the past hour.

Danny heard Fred and climbed down a few branches. He moved quickly and easily without falling.

"What are you doing, Fred?" he asked in a friendly voice.

"I was just finishing up my lunch," Fred answered. "How is life up high today, my friend?"

"It's wonderful!" Danny announced. He loved being a tree frog. He felt lucky to be able to climb this way and that. He had sticky pads on his hands and feet.

"I noticed today that my skin is the same color as these leaves. I had a great hiding spot!" Danny told Fred.

"Well, it is too bad I can't hop up there to play hide-and-seek with you, Danny," Fred said.

Sometimes Fred wished he could get up in the tree like Danny. Fred was a great jumper with powerful hind legs, but he couldn't climb trees. He was much too big.

As Danny kept talking about his day, Fred felt himself getting upset. He didn't want to hear any more about life as a tree frog. Fred yelled up in an angry voice, "Danny, could you be quiet up there? You're giving me a headache!"

"Oh, I'm sorry," Danny said. He felt sad and hurt. He sat quietly.

Fred sat by the pond and felt bad about what he had said. Danny was always excited about everything. It was what Fred liked most about him.

Just as Fred was about to apologize, he felt a cold shadow fall over him. Then he heard Danny's warning call.

Fred leapt forward at once. He disappeared safely into the deep pond just as a large bird tried to grab him. The bird flew away. Danny sat very still in his tree.

"Thanks, Danny," Fred said.

"You're welcome, Fred," Danny said. "Can you show me that jump again? I wish I could jump that far. My legs aren't as strong as your legs."

"We all have something that makes us special, don't we?" Fred smiled.

Frogs

Frogs are amphibians. This means they live part of their life in water and part on land. Frogs begin life as tadpoles in the water. They breathe through gills like fish. The tadpoles grow into frogs. They lose their tail and gills, and they grow legs and lungs. Now they are adult frogs that live and breathe on land.

Like all living things, frogs need air, food, and water to live. They eat insects, worms, and snails. Frogs also shed their skin as they grow. Then they eat it!

Bullfrog tadpole